Magical Herbal
Baths
of Santeria

Carlos Galdiano Montenegro

ORIGINAL PUBLICATIONS
New York

MAGICAL HERBAL BATHS OF SANTERIA
© 1996 by ORIGINAL PUBLICATIONS

ISBN: 0-942272-45-5

Original Publications
P.O. Box 236
Old Bethpage, New York 11804-0236
1-888-OCCULT-1

Printed in the United States of America

DEDICATION

This book is dedicated to the Orishas and to
my Mother and Father.
With love and respect.

ACHE

Carlos Galdiano Montenegro

TABLE OF CONTENTS

INTRODUCTION

The birth of Santeria took place in the 1600's when Yoruba families were displaced from their Nigerian homeland and were brought to work as slaves on the Spanish plantations in Cuba and Puerto Rico. The new inhabitants carried with them to the Caribbean a very powerful and complex religion from Africa. In order for the religion to survive and to avoid persecution from the Roman Catholic plantation owners, they were able to secretly incorporate their beliefs and customs within the Roman Catholic religion.

The leaders of the African-based religion are called Santeros. A Santero Priest carries the ancient knowledge and wisdom of the powerful African deities known collectively as Orishas. An experienced Santero is a great herbalist and also knows the secrets to very powerful African magic. Presently, it has been estimated that there are over 20 million practitioners and followers of Santeria in the world. The vast majority of Santeria practitioners in the United States are located in New York City, Miami and Los Angeles. In the city of Los Angeles, there are more than 600 Santeria house worship centers where practitioners secretly and discretely practice the ancient traditions of Santeria.

In 1993, the Supreme Court of the United States established Santeria as a legitimate and legal religion. Although Santeria has been accepted by the government of the United States, the powerful initiations and spiritual remedies are still guarded secrets of the powerful Santero Priests.

The future of Santeria seems very bright and positive. Santeria is spreading across America and Europe at a rapid rate, attracting followers and practitioners of many different ethnic backgrounds. One of the reasons that Santeria has become so popular is due to the use of natural remedies and herbal medicines prepared by the Santero Priests. By combinin elements of spirituality with that of nature, a Santero Priest can accomplish great success with even the most difficult case. Spiritual herbal baths are widely used in the Santeria Religion. Although all of the ingredients are natural, when combined with powerful supernatural magic, these herbal baths can produce incredible results.

5

Modern day scientists have not been able to explain this but perhaps someday the cure for the common cold or even many terminal illnesses such as cancer and AIDS might be found in one of Santeria's magical herbs or spiritual remedies.

In the beginning, Olodumare created man.
He placed the plants and trees in the Garden of Eden
to heal and to protect all those who serve and glorify
His sacred name.

CARLOS GALDIANO MONTENEGRO

BITTER HERB BATHS

A bitter herb bath is made from herbs that spiritually repel negative energy. Many Spiritualists and Santeros use a bitter herb bath to rid themselves or others from unwanted negative vibrations. Following a bitter bath, an individual will take a sweet herb bath to draw in positive spiritual energies.

BITTER HERBS

1. ALAMU
2. ANAMU
3. APOSOTE
4. ABRE CAMINO
5. CORTADERA
6. ESPARTILLO
7. ESCOBA AMARGA
8. HEDIONDA
9. LENGUA DE VACA
10. PATA DE GALLINA
11. QUITA MALDICION
12. ROMPE ZARAGUEY
13. RUDA
14. SALVADERA
15. TARTAGO
16. ROMERO
17. YERBA BUENA
18. ZARZAPARILLA

BITTER HERB BATH #1

This bitter herb bath should be used by an individual that has been bewitched.

INGREDIENTS

1. RUDA
2. ROMERO
3. KOSHER ROCK SALT
4. HOLY WATER
5. FLORIDA WATER

PREPARATION

1. Boil the Ruda and the Romero in one gallon of water
2. Allow the mixture to cool.
3. Strain the liquid from the mixture into a large bowl.
4. Add the Kosher Rock Salt to the liquid mixture.
5. Add the Holy Water to the liquid mixture.
6. Add the Florida Water to the liquid mixture.
7. Pour the liquid mixture into your bath water.

Remain in the bath water for 30 minutes. Take this bath for three consecutive days. Follow all bitter herb baths with a sweet herb bath.

BITTER HERB BATH #2

This bitter herb bath is used to discharge the negative energies surrounding a person.

INGREDIENTS

1. BASIL
2. HOLY WATER
3. CASCARILLA
4. REVERSE CANDLE

PREPARATION

1. Boil the Basil in one gallon of water.
2. Allow the mixture to cool.
3. Strain the liquid from the mixture into a large bowl.
4. Add the Holy Water to the liquid mixture.
5. Add the Cascarilla to the liquid mixture.
6. Pour the liquid mixture into your bath water

Remain in the bath water for 30 minutes. Light the Reverse Candle after taking the bath. This bath should be taken for three consecutive days, followed each day with a sweet herb bath.

BITTER HERB BATH #3

This bitter herb bath is used when an individual is so badly bewitched that their life may be in danger. This bitter herb bath will remove very strong and powerful witchcraft.

INGREDIENTS

1. MIRTO
2. POMEGRANATE JUICE
3. GOAT'S MILK
4. KOSHER ROCK SALT
5. HOLY WATER
6. CASCARILLA

PREPARATION

1. Pour the Goat's Milk into a large bowl.
2. Add the Pomegranate Juice into the Goat's Milk.
3. Add the Holy Water to the liquid mixture.
4. Add the Cascarilla to the liquid mixture.
5. Pour your bath water.
6. Stand up in the bath water
7. Pour the entire mixture over your head

BITTER BATH #3 (CONTINUED)

Remain soaking in the bath water for 30 minutes. This powerful bath should be taken for three to five consecutive days. Follow with three consecutive sweet herb baths.

BITTER HERB BATH #4

This bitter herb bath is taken by an individual to get rid of negative people that are causing you problems.

INGREDIENTS

1. ROMERO
2. ESPARTILLO
3. GARLIC
4. FLORIDA WATER
5. HOLY WATER

PREPARATION

1. Boil the Garlic, Romero and the Espartillo in one gallon of water.
2. Allow the Liquid mixture to cool.
3. Strain the liquid from the mixture into a large bowl.
4. Add the Florida Water to the liquid mixture.
5. Add the Holy Water to the liquid mixture.
6. Pour the liquid mixture into your bath water.

Remain in the water for 30 minutes. This bath should be taken for three consecutive days.

BITTER HERB BATH #5

This bitter herb bath should be taken by an individual when they feel that they have been exposed to negative forces and vibrations.

INGREDIENTS

1. KOSHER ROCK SALT   2. LIME JUICE   3. HOLY WATER

PREPARATION

1. Pour the Lime Juice into a large bowl

2. Add the Kosher Rock Salt to the Lime Juice.
3. Add the Holy Water to the liquid mixture.
4. Pour the liquid mixture into your bath water.

Remain in the bath for 30 minutes. This bitter herb bath should be taken for five consecutive days.

SWEET HERB BATHS

A Sweet Herb Bath is used to bring an individual positive energy and prosperity. A Sweet Herb Bath is used after a Bitter Herb Bath.

SWEET HERBS

1. ALBAHACA
2. BERRO
3. BOTON DE ORO
4. CANELA
5. CARNATIONS
6. FLOR DE AGUA

7. LILAC
8. LAVENDER
9. MENTA
10. MIRTO
11. MANZANILLA
12. MARAVILLA

13. MEJORANA
14. ROSES
15. SALVIA
16. VERBENA
17. YERBA BUENA

SWEET HERB BATH #1

INGREDIENTS

1. BOTON DE ORO
2. VERBENA

3. WHITE CARNATIONS
4. HOLY WATER

PREPARATION

1. Boil the Boton De Oro and the Verbena in one gallon of water.
2. Allow the liquid mixture to cool, then strain into a large bowl.
3. Place the petals from the White Carnations into the mixture.
4. Add the Holy Water to the mixture.
5. Pour the mixture into your bath water.

Remain in the bath water for 30 minutes. Take this Sweet Herb Bath for three consecutive days.

SWEET HERB BATH #2

INGREDIENTS

1. ALBAHACA
2. MIRTO
3. CINNAMON STICKS
4. FLORIDA WATER
5. HOLY WATER

PREPARATION

1. Boil the Albahaca, Mirto and the Cinnamon Sticks in one gallon of water.
2. Allow the mixture to cool.
3. Strain the liquid from the mixture into a large bowl.
4. Add the Florida Water to the mixture
5. Add the Holy Water to the liquid mixture.
6. Pour the liquid mixture into your bath

Remain in your bath water for 30 minutes. Take this sweet herb bath for three consecutive days.

SWEET HERB BATH #3

INGREDIENTS

1. LILAC FLOWERS
2. MILK
3. AGUA DE COCO
4. AGUA DE ROSAS
5. HOLY WATER

PREPARATION

1. Boil the Lilac Flowers in one gallon of water.
2. Allow the mixture to cool.
3. Strain the liquid from the mixture into a large bowl.
4. Add the Agua de Coco to the liquid mixture.
5. Add the Agua de Rosas to the liquid mixture.
6. Add the Holy Water to the liquid mixture.
7. Pour the liquid mixture into your bath water.

Remain in the bath water for 30 minutes. Take this sweet herb bath for three consecutive days.

12

SWEET HERB BATH #4

INGREDIENTS

1. SUNFLOWER PETALS
2. ACHE DE SANTO
3. AGUA DE COCO
4. HOLY WATER
5. KOLONIA 1800

PREPARATION

1. Cut up the petals of the Sunflower into small fine pieces.
2. Place the Sunflower pieces into a large bowl.
3. Add the Holy Water to the Sunflower mixture.
4. Add the Agua de Coco to the liquid mixture.
5. Add the Ache de Santo to the liquid mixture.
6. Add the Kolonia 1800 to the liquid mixture
7. Pour the liquid mixture into your bath water.

Remain in the bath water for 30 minutes. Take this sweet herb bath for two consecutive days.

SWEET HERB BATH #5

INGREDIENTS

1. MENTA
2. WHITE ROSES
3. LAVENDER WATER
4. HOLY WATER
5. WHITE CANDLE

PREPARATION

1. Cut up the petals from the Roses into small pieces.
2. Cut up the Menta into small fine pieces.
3. Place the pieces of the cut Rose petals & the Menta into a large bowl.
4. Pour the Lavender Water over the herbal mixture.
5. Add the Holy Water to the mixture and pour into the bath water.
6. Light the White Candle.

Remain in the bath water for 30 minutes. Take this bath for three consecutive days.

13

ELEGGUA

The Orisha Eleggua is the Divine Messenger of the Orishas. The Orisha Eleggua is the keeper of the crossroads and it is through him that all magic begins.

HERBS SACRED TO ELEGGUA

1. ABRE CAMINO
2. ALACRANCILLO
3. ARRASA
4. AJI PICANTE
5. ALMACIGO DE CUARTO CAMINOS
6. AGUIMALDO
7. ATEJE
8. BOTON DE ORO
9. BARRIGUILLA
10. BELO
11. CASCARA DE COCO
12. COROJO
13. CAFE
14. ESPARTILLO
15. GUAYABA
16. GUARO
17. GANDUL
18. GUACALOTE
19. HORTIGUILLA
20. HEDIODONDA
21. HIERBA MENTIROSA
22. HOJAS DEL FRIJOL DE CARITA
23. HOJAS DE AGUACATE
24. ITAMO REAL
25. LENGUA DE VACA
26. LLAMAO
27. MENTA
28. MASTUERZO
29. MALOJA
30. MELONCILLO
31. ORILLE
32. PICA PICA
33. PENDEJERA
34. PINON BLANCA
35. PATA DE GALLINA
36. PINGA HERMOSA
37. PINON CRIOLLO
38. PASTILLO
39. RABO DE ZORRA
40. SALTA PERICO
41. SALGASO
42. RAIZ DE AGUACATE
43. TRAVESURA
44. TALLO DE MAIZ
45. VARIA
46. VENTE COMIGO
47. YERBA FINA

ELEGGUA ROAD OPENER BATH

This bath is used by an individual to open up the roads to opportunity and success.

INGREDIENTS

1. ABRE CAMINO
2. MENTA
3. GUAYABA
4. ALBAHACA
5. AGUADIENTE
6. KOLONIA 1800
7. HOLY WATER
8. WHITE CANDLE

PREPARATION

1. Boil the Abre Camino, Guayaba, Menta and the Albahaca in one gallon of water.
2. Allow the liquid mixture to cool.
3. Strain the liquid from the large mixture into a large bowl.
4. Add the Holy Water to the liquid mixture.
5. Add the Aguardiente to the liquid mixture
6. Add the Kolonia 1800 to the liquid mixture.
7. Light the candle in honor of Eleggua.
8. Pour the liquid mixture into your bath water.

Remain in the bath water for 30 minutes. This bath should be started on Mondays and taken for three consecutive days.

ELEGGUA REVERSE BATH

Another popular bath for Eleggua is the reverse bath. This bath is taken by an individual who has been the target of witchcraft or the evil eye.

INGREDIENTS

1. GUAYABA
2. MASTURZO
3. ESPARTILLO
4. KOSHER ROCK SALT
5. CASCARILLA
6. HOLY WATER
7. FLORIDA WATER
8. REVERSE CANDLE

PREPARATION

1. Boil the Guayaba, Masturzo, Espartillo and the Kosher Rock Salt in one gallon of water.
2. Allow the liquid mixture to cool.
3. Strain the liquid from the mixture into a large bowl.
4. Add the Florida Water to the liquid mixture.
5. Add the Holy Water to the liquid mixture.
6. Add the Cascarilla to the liquid mixture.
7. Pour the liquid mixture into your bath water.

Light the Reverse Candle and remain in the bath water for 30 minutes. Most Santeros recommend taking this bath for three consecutive days followed by three consecutive sweet baths.

ELEGGUA RETURN BATH

INGREDIENTS

1. ABRE CAMINO	6. WHITE CANDLE
2. VENTE COMIGO	7. CIGAR
3. MENTE	8. SMALL BOTTLE OF RUM
4. AGUA DE COCO	9. SMALL DISH OF CANDIES
5. SIETE MACHOS WATER	

PREPARATION

1. Boil the Abre Camino, Menta and the Vente Comigo in one gallon of water.
2. Allow the liquid mixture to cool.
3. Strain the liquid from the mixture into a large bowl.
4. Add the Agua de Coco to the liquid mixture.
5. Add the Siete Machos Water to the liquid mixture.
6. Light the candle in honor of Eleggua.
7. Place the offerings next to the candle (Cigar, Candies, and the Rum)
8. Pour the liquid mixture into your bath water.

Remain in the bath water for 30 minutes. This bath should be started on Monday and taken for five consecutive days.

OBATALA

The Orisha Obatala is known as the "Father of Purity" and white light. The Orisha Obatala is associated with healing and with cleansing ceremonies.

HERBS SACRED TO OBATALA

1. Algodon	8. Guanabana	15. Peregun
2. Almendra	9. Flor de Agua	16. Prodigiosa
3. Aguinaldo Blanco	10. Huiguereta	17. Peonia
4. Bleo Blanco	11. Jagua Blanca	18. Sauco Blanco
5. Campana Blanca	12. Lirio Blanco	19. San Diego
6. Canutillo Blanco	13. Mata de Pincho	20. Vergolaga
7. Eguere Tete	14. Malva	

OBATALA CLEANSING BATH

This bath is used to purify an individual who has experienced great difficulties in their life.

INGREDIENTS

1. ABRE CAMINO
2. VENTE COMIGO
3. MENTE
6. WHITE CANDLE
7. CIGAR

PREPARATION

1. Remove the petals from the Flor de Agua and cut them up into small fine pieces.
2. Mix the Agua de Coco, Cascarilla and the Florida Water in one gallon of fresh water.
3. Add the Flor de Agua to the liquid mixture.
4. Light the candle in honor of Obatala
5. Allow the liquid mixture to stand for 24 hours.
6. After the 24 hours, pour the liquid mixture into your bath water.

Remain in the bath water for 30 minutes. This bath should be taken once a week for one calendar month.

OBATALA CLEANSING BATH

This bath is used to purify your aura after a ceremony or magic ritual.

INGREDIENTS

1. CAMPANA BLANCA
2. MILK
3. HOLY WATER
4. CASCARILLA
5. KOLONIA 1800
6. WHITE CANDLE

PREPARATION

1. Remove the petals from the Campana Blanca and cut them up into small fine pieces.
2. Mix the Holy Water, Milk and Kolonia 1800 into one gallon of fresh water.
3. Add the Campana Blanca into the liquid mixture.
4. Light the candle in honor of Obatala.
5. Pour the liquid mixture into your bath water.

Remain in the bath water for 30 minutes. After the bath, rub the Cascarilla in the form of a cross on the bottom of both feet and the palms of your hands.

CHANGO

The Orisha Chango is known in Santeria as the God of Thunder, Power and War. Baths taken with the sacred herbs of Chango are for individuals who want to have great power and victory over their enemies.

HERBS SACRED TO CHANGO

1. ALAMO
2. ALMACIGO
3. AJO DE GOMA
4. AMANSA GUAPO
5. ARTEMISAS
6. AJO VEGETAL
7. BLEDO PUNZO
8. CANUTILLO ROJO
9. GRANADA
10. GUAYACAN
11. HUEVO DE TORO
12. JOBO
13. MAMEY
14. MANZANA
15. MOCO DE PAVO
16. PARAISO
17. PITALLA
18. PLATANO
19. PINO
20. PALMA REAL
21. PALO BOBO
22. PINO DE BOTIJA
23. RUDA
24. ROMPE ZARAGUEY
25. SANTA BARBARA
26. SALVADERA
27. SIGUARAYA
28. TREPADERA
29. TUATUA
30. VACABUEY
31. ZARZAPARILLA

CHANGO POWER BATH

INGREDIENTS

1. PARAISO
2. GRANADA
3. SIETE MACHOS WATER
4. PRECIPITADO RADO
5. RED CANDLE

PREPARATION

1. Boil the Paraiso in one gallon of water.
2. Allow the mixture to cool.
3. Strain the liquid from the mixture into a large bowl.

4. Pulverize the inside fruit of the Granada into a liquid.
5. Add the Granada juice to the liquid mixture.
6. Add the Siete Machos Water to the liquid mixture.
7. Dress the candle with the Precipitado Rojo.
8. Light the candle in honor of Chango.
9. Pour the liquid into your bath water.

Remain in the bath water for 30 minutes. This bath should be taken on Fridays.

CHANGO CLEANSING BATH

This bath will protect an individual who is in extreme danger.

INGREDIENTS

1. ZARZAPARILLA
2. GRANADA
3. KOSHER ROCK SALT
4. MILK
5. CASCARILLA
6. RED CANDLE

PREPARATION

1. Boil the Zarzaparilla in one gallon of water.
2. Allow the mixture to cool.
3. Strain the liquid from the mixture into a large bowl.
4. Pulverize the inside fruit of the Granada into a liquid.
5. Add the Granada juice to the liquid mixture.
6. Add the Milk to the liquid mixture.
7. Add the Kosher Rock Salt to the liquid mixture.
8. Light the candle in honor of Chango.
9. Pour the liquid mixture into your bath water.

Remain in the bath water for 30 minutes. This bath should be taken for three consecutive days. Rub the Cascarilla in the form of a cross on the bottom of both feet.

CHANGO LOVE BATH

The Orisha Chango is also known as a great lover. This bath is used by men to attract a woman. A super strong magical bath.

INGREDIENTS

1. HOJA DE GUAYABA
2. AMANSA GUAPO
3. SIETE MACHOS WATER
4. YOUR FAVORITE COLOGNE
5. HONEY
6. RED CANDLE

PREPARATION

Boil the Hoja de Guayaba and the Amansa Guapo in one gallon of water.
Strain the hot liquid from the mixture into a large bowl.
Add the Honey to the liquid mixture.
Add the Siete Machos Water to the liquid mixture.
Add your favorite Cologne to the liquid mixture.
Light the candle in Honor of Chango.
Pour the liquid mixture into your bath water.

Remain in the bath water for 30 minutes. This bath should be taken before going out for the evening.

OCHUN

The Orisha Ochun is the Venus of the Santeria Religion. An individual would take a bath in Ochun's sacred herbs when they desire love, money and wealth.

HERBS SACRED TO OCHUN

1. ALAMBRILLA
2. AMBAR
3. ANIS
4. ACHIVATA
5. ARABITO
6. BOTON DE ORO
7. BERRO
8. COLONIA
9. CUCARACHA
10. CERRAJA
11. CULANTRILLA
12. DIEZ DEL DIA
13. FLOR DE AGUA
14. FELIGRAMA
15. FRESCURA
16. GUASIMA
17. HIERBA ANIL
18. HIERBA BUENA
19. HIERBA DE LA NINA
20. HIERBA FINA
21. HUEVO DE GALLO
22. HOJAS DE NARANJA
23. HELENCHO
24. LECHUGA
25. LLANTEN
26. LINO DE MAR
27. MARAVILLA
28. MAZORQUILLA
29. MARILOPE
30. MASTUERZO
31. ORASUN
32. PARAQUITA MORADA
33. PALO DE CANELA
34. PALO DULCE
35. PANETELA
36. ROSAS AMARILLOS
37. ROMERO
38. UVA MORADA
39. VERBENA

OCHUN LOVE BATH

This bath is taken by an individual who wants to attract the opposite sex.

INGREDIENTS

1. YELLOW ROSES
2. ROMAINE LETTUCE
3. HONEY
4. ROSE WATER
5. RIVER WATER
6. YELLOW CANDLE

PREPARATION

1. Boil the petals of the Yellow Roses in one gallon of water.
2. Allow the mixture to cool
3. Strain the liquid from the mixture into a large bowl.
4. Add the Honey to the liquid mixture.
5. Add the River Water to the liquid mixture.
6. Add the Rose water to the liquid mixture.
7. Cut the Romaine Lettuce into small pieces and mix into the liquid mixture.
8. Light the candle in honor of Ochun.
9. Pour the liquid mixture into your bath water.

Remain in the bath water for 30 minutes. This bath should be taken for five consecutive days.

OCHUN LOVE BATH

This is a very strong attraction bath that usually has fast results.

INGREDIENTS

1. HOJAS DE NARANJA
2. FLOR DE AGUA
3. HONEY
4. CINNAMON STICKS
5. YELLOW ROSES
6. RIVER WATER
7. FOUR SMALL YELLOW CANDLES

PREPARATION

1. Boil the Cinnamon Sticks, Hojas de Naranja and the Honey in one gallon of water.
2. Allow the mixture to cool.
3. Strain the liquid from the mixture into a large bowl.
4. Add the River Water to the mixture.
5. Cut the petals of the Yellow Roses and the Flor de Agua into small fine pieces.
6. Add the cut flower pieces to the mixture.
7. Place the four yellow candles around the outside of the bowl with the liquid mixture.

8. Light the candles in honor of Ochun.
9. When the candles have completely burned out,
   pour the liquid mixture into your bath water.

Remain in the bath water for 30 minutes. This bath should be taken for five consecutive days.

OCHUN'S SEDUCTION BATH

This is a traditional bath used by women who work at bars or as prostitutes. The power of this bath is used to seduce a man into giving a woman all of his money.

INGREDIENTS

1. CINNAMON STICKS
2. MILK
3. BROWN SUGAR
4. ROMAINE LETTUCE
5. HONEY
6. YOUR FAVORITE PERFUME
7. YELLOW CANDLE

PREPARATIONS

1. Boil the Cinnamon Sticks, Honey and Brown
2. Sugar in one gallon of water.
3. Allow the mixture to cool.
4. Strain the mixture into a large bowl.
5. Add your favorite perfume to the liquid mixture.
6. Cut the Romaine Lettuce into small pieces and add it to the liquid mixture.
7. Light the candle in honor of Ochun.
8. Pour the mixture into your bath water.

Remain in the bath water for 30 minutes. This bath should be taken at night.

OCHUN'S MONEY BATH

This bath is used to attract money, success in business or to receive a raise in salary.

INGREDIENTS

1. ANIS
2. HIERBA BUENA
3. BROWN MUSTARD SEEDS
4. CINNAMON STICKS
5. FLORIDA WATER
6. YELLOW CANDLE

PREPARATIONS

1. Boil the Anis, Hierba Buena, Cinnamon Sticks and the Brown Mustard Seed in one gallon of water.
2. Allow the mixture to cool.
3. Strain the liquid from the mixture into a large bowl.
4. Add the Florida Water to the Liquid mixture.
5. Light the candle in Honor of Ochun.
6. Pour the liquid mixture into your bath water.

Remain in the bath water for 30 minutes. This bath should be taken on Sundays.

OCHUN'S RELATIONSHIP BATH

This bath is used to seduce your spouse or lover and to bring back sex to your marriage or love affair.

INGREDIENTS

1. CINNAMON STICKS
2. MARAVILLA
3. DAMIANA
4. PALO DULCE
5. HONEY
6. AGUA DE ROSAS
7. RIVER WATER
8. YELLOW CANDLE

25

PREPARATIONS

1. Boil the Cinnamon Sticks, Maravilla, Palo Dulce, Damiana and the Honey in one gallon of water.
2. Allow the mixture to cool.
3. Strain the liquid from the mixture into a large bowl.
4. Add the River Water to the liquid mixture.
5. Add the Agua de Rosas to the liquid mixture.
6. Light the candle in honor of Ochun.
7. Pour the liquid mixture into your bath water.

Remain in the bath water for 30 minutes. This bath should be taken for three consecutive days. For extra strength, Santeros recommend placing a small piece of Palo Dulce in your favorite perfume or cologne.

YEMAYA

The Orisha Yemaya is the Great Mother of the World. Yemaya is the Goddess of the Seven Seas. The Orishas are generally associated with fertility and bringing peace and happiness to an individual.

HERBS SACRED TO YEMAYA

1. ANIL
2. ANAMU
3. ALGA MARINA
4. ALBAHACA MORADA
5. AJI
6. BERRO
7. CHAYOTE
8. CHINZOSA
9. ESPONJA
10. FLOR DEL MAR
11. GRAMA DE LA PLAYA
12. HELENCHO
13. HIERBA BUENA
14. HIERBA FLORIDA
15. JUNCOS DEL MAR
16. LECHUGA
17. MAJAGUA
18. PALO DULCE
19. SANDIA

YEMAYA'S TRANQUILITY BATH

This bath brings a person great inner peace and clarity of mind.

INGREDIENTS

1. ALBAHACA MORADA
2. CHAYOTE
3. CASCARILLA
4. SEA WATER
5. KOLONIA 1800
6. AGUA DE COCO
7. BLUE CANDLE

PREPARATION

1. Boil the Albahaca Morada and the Chayote in one gallon of water.
2. Allow the mixture to cool.
3. Strain the liquid from the mixture into a large bowl.
4. Add the Agua de Coco to the liquid mixture.

5. Add the Kolonia 1800 to the liquid mixture.
6. Add the Cascarilla to the liquid mixture.
7. Light the Blue Candle.
8. Pour the liquid mixture into your bath water.

Remain in the bath water for 30 minutes. This bath should be taken for three consecutive nights before going to bed.

YEMAYA'S FERTILITY BATH

This is a popular and traditional bath for women who want to achieve pregnancy.

INGREDIENTS

1. SANDIA
2. SEA WATER
3. FLOR DEL MAR
4. FLOR DE AGUA
5. FLORIDA WATER
6. SEVEN PANNIES
7. BLUE CANDLE

PREPARATION

1. Cut the petals of the Flor del mar and the Flor de Agua into small pieces.
2. Place the cut petals of both flowers into a large bowl.
3. Pour the Sea Water over the flower petals.
4. Add the Florida Water to the liquid mixture.
5. Cut a small hole in the Sandia and place the
6. seven pennies inside.
   Place the liquid mixture next to the sandia.
7. Light the candle in honor of Yemaya.
8. Allow the liquid mixture to stand for three days.
9. On the third day, pour the liquid mixture into your bath water.

Remain in the bath water for 30 minutes. This bat should be taken once a week. Take the Sandia to the ocean as an offering to Yemaya. This is a very powerful fertility bath and the Orisha Yemaya is fast to respond to your requests.

YEMAYA'S FERTILITY BATH

This bath is taken by individuals seeking the protection of Yemaya and also for special requests.

INGREDIENTS

1. BERRO
2. YERBA BUENA
3. SEA WATER
4. VIOLET WATER
5. BLUE CANDLE

PREPARATION

1. Cut the Berro and the Yerba Buena into fine small pieces.
2. Place the herbs in a large bowl.
3. Pour the Sea Water over the herbal mixture.
4. Add the Violet Water to the liquid mixture.
5. Light the candle in honor of Yemaya.
6. Pour the liquid mixture into your abth water.

Remain in the bath water for 30 minutes. This bath should be taken for seven consecutive days.

OLOCUN

The orisha Olocun is associated with the mysteries of the deep oceans. Baths taken with Olocun's sacred herbs gives an individual great stability in life. The Orisha Olocun also brungs great success to individuals involved in business.

HERBS SACRED TO OLOCUN

1. ANIL
2. ANAMU
3. ALGA MARINA
4. ALBAHACA
5. AJI
6. BERRO
7. CHAYOTE
8. CHINZOSA
9. ESPONJA
10. FLOR DEL MAR
11. HELENCHO
12. HIERBA BUENA
13. HIERBA FLORIDA
14. JUNCOS DEL MAR
15. LECHUGA
16. MAJAGUA
17. PALO DULCE
18. SANDIA

OLOCUN'S STABILITY BATH

This bath is used by individuals who are confused and need direction in their life.

INGREDIENTS

1. FLOR DEL MAR
2. SEA WATER
3. ACHE DE SANTO
4. KOLONIA 1800
5. BLUE CANDLE

PREPARATION

1. Boil the Flor del Mar and the Ache de Santo in one gallon of water.
2. Allow the mixture to cool.
3. Add the Kolonia 1800 to the liquid mixture.
4. Pour the liquid mixture into your bath water.

Remain in the bath water for 30 minutes. Take this bath for seven consecutive days. Some Santeros recommend placing a small silver ankle bracelet with an anchor on your left foot after the seven days of this bath.

OLOCUN'S BUSINESS BATH

This bath should be taken by an individual seeking the strength of Olocun in business.

INGREDIENTS

1. FLOR DEL MAR
2. ANIL
3. SEA WATER
4. WHITE FLOWER PETALS
5. FOUR SMALL BLUE CANDLES
6. SIETE MACHOS WATER

PREPARATION

1. Place the Flor de Mar and the White Flower Petals in a large bowl.
2. Pour the Sea Waterand the Siete Machos Water over the flower petals.
3. Place a small ball of Anil into the liquid mixture.
4. Place the four small blue candles around the outside of the bowl.
5. Light the candles in honor of Olocun.
6. Allow the candles to completely burn out.
7. After the candles have finished burning out, pour the liquid mixture into your bath water.

Remain in the bath water for 30 minutes. This bath should be taken once a week.

ORISHA OKO

The Orisha Oko is associated with agriculture and the harvest of the land. Orisha Oko is associated with men and fertility.

VEGETABLES AND GRAINS
SACRED TO OKO

1. CORN
2. BLACK BEANS
3. RED BEANS
4. PINTO BEANS
5. KIDNEY BEANS
6. GARBONZO BEANS
7. GANDULES
8. SUGAR CANE
9. OKRA
10. EGGPLANT
11. LIMA BEANS
12. WHITE BEANS
13. CARROTS
14. CABBAGE
15. LETTUCE
16. KALE
17. BEETS
18. RICE
19. TOMATOES
20. POTATOES
21. WHEAT
22. RADISHES
23. JICAMA
24. YUCA
25. CELERY

ORISHA OKO LEADERSHIP BATH

The following bath is for men only. This bath will bring strong leadership abilities and strengthen your role as a male in society.

INGREDIENTS

1. FRESH CORN
2. FRESH PIGEON PEAS
3. SIETE MACHOS WATER
4. HOLY WATER
5. AGUARDIENTE
6. YELLOW CANDLE

PREPARATION

1. Place the Fresh Corn kernals and the Pigeon Peas in a large mixing bowl.
2. Pour the Holy Water over the vegetables.
3. Add the Siete Machos Water to the liquid mixture.

4. Add the Aguardiente to the liquid mixture.
5. Light the candle in honor of Orisha Oko.
6. Pour the liquid mixture into your bath water.

Remain in the bath water for 30 minutes. This bath should be taken for four consecutive days.

ORISHA OKO'S FERTILITY BATH

This is a special bath for men who desire to have a male child. This bath is called a Dry Bath in Santeria and therefore it requires the use of the earth. This bath must be done outside.

INGREDIENTS

1. DRY BLACK BEANS
2. DRY RED BEANS
3. DRY KIDNEY BEANS
4. DRY GARBANZO BEANS
5. DRY LIMA BEANS
6. DRY WHITE BEANS
7. RICE
8. CIGAR
9. BOTTLE OF RUM
10. SMALL YELLOW CANDLE

PREPARATION

1. Dig a shallow hole, large enough to stand in, in the ground.
2. Mix all of the dry grains together in a large bowl.
3. Light the cigar and blow the smoke in the hole.
4. Stand in the shallow hole and begin to pray to Orisha Oko for your request of a male child.
5. While praying, pour the entire grain mixture over your head.
6. Step out of the hole.
7. Place the remainder of the Cigar in the hole.
8. Pour the Rum into the hole.
9. Cover the grain and the hole with earth.
10. Form a mound with the earth.
11. Place the yellow candle in the center of the mound.
12. Light the candle in honor of Orisha Oko.

BABALU-AYE

The Orisha Babalu-Aye is known in Santeria as the "Great Healer". Babalu-Aye has been known to practitioners of Santeria to heal many incurable diseases.

HERBS SACRED TO BABALU-AYE

1. APAZOTE	16. JAYABICO
2. ATEJE	17. MANI
3. ALACRANCILLA	18. MARIPOSA
4. ANGARIYA	19. LLAMAGUA
5. AJONJOLI	20. OLIVO
6. CUNDIAMOR	21. PICA PICA
7. CAISIMON	22. ROSA DE JERICO
8. CAMPANA MORADA	23. RETAMO
9. ESCOBA AMARGA	24. SALVIA
10. FRIJOLES	25. TENGUE TENGUE
11. GUAGUSI	26. TAPA CAMINO
12. HIERBA NINA	27. TUNA
13. HIERBA VIEJA	28. YALLA
14. HABEY	29. ZARGOZO
15. HENEQUEY	30. ZAZAFRAN

BABALU-AYE HEALING BATH #1

This bath is used in Santeria to heal an individual with a sickness.

INGREDIENTS

1. SALVIA	4. CASCARILLA
2. HIERBA NINA	5. AGUA DECOROJO
3. KOLONIA 1800	6. MANTECA DECOROJO

PREPARATION

1. Boil the Salvia, Hierba Nina and the Manteca de Corojo in one gallon of water.
2. Allow the mixture to cool.
3. Strain the liquid from the mixture into a large bowl.
4. Add the Agua de Coco to the liquid mixture.
5. Add the Kolonia 1800 to the liquid mixture.
6. Light the candle in honor of Babalu-Aye.
7. Pour the liquid mixture into your bath water.

Remain in the bath water for 30 minutes. Santeros recommend taking this bath once a week. A person with a terminal illness should take this bath for seven consecutive days.

BABALU-AYE HEALING BATH #2

This bath is used by an individual to prevent illness and disease.

INGREDIENTS

1. EGGPLANT
2. SALVIA
3. RUDA
4. AGUARDIENTE
5. CASCARILLA
6. FLORIDA WATER

PREPARATION

1. Cut the Eggplant into small pieces and place them into a large bowl.
2. Boil the Salvia and the Ruda in one gallon of water.
3. Strain the liquid from the mixture into the large bowl with the Eggplant pieces.
4. Add the Florida Water to the Liquid mixture.
5. Add the Aguardiente to the liquid mixture.
6. Add the Cascarilla to the liquid mixture.
7. Light the candle in honor of Babalu-Aye.
8. Pour the liquid mixture into your bath water.

Remain in the bath water for 30 minutes. This bath should be taken once a week. The preferred day for this bath is Wednesday.

BABALU-AYE DRY BATH

This dry bath to Babalu-Aye is said to prevent death and tragic accidents.

INGREDIENTS

1. SEVEN WHITE PLATES
2. BLACK BEANS
3. LIMA BEANS
4. RED BEANS
5. GARBONZO BEANS
6. CHOPPED APPLES
7. CHOPPED PEARS
8. HONEY
9. BOTTLE OF RUM
10. CIGAR
11. ONE SMALL PURPLE CANDLE

PREPARATION

1. Dig a shallow hole large enough to stand in.
2. On each of the seven white plates, place one of the ingredients listed above.
3. Light the cigar and blow smoke into the hole, about three times.
4. Stand in the hole.
5. Pass each of the plates of vegetables and fruits over your body.
6. Empty the vegetables and fruits into the hole as you pass them over your body.
7. Step out of the hole.
8. After you have finished the cleansing, pour the Rum in the hole over the vegetables and fruits.
9. Cover the hole with a mound of dirt.
10. Place the candle in the middle of the mound.
11. Light the candle in honor of Babalu-Aye.

This dry cleansing bath should be taken once a month or when you feel death is near.

ORUNLA

The Orisha Orunla is known in Santeria as the "Great Diviner". The Orisha Orunla has the powers of prophecy and spiritual communication. An individual would take a bath in Orunla's sacred herbs to bring clarity of mind and powers of spiritual communication.

HERBS SACRED TO ORUNLA

1. BASTON DE ORUNLA
2. CHINCHITA
3. COPEY
4. COOLOZO
5. GALAN DE NOCHE
6. GUASIMITO
7. GENGIBRE
8. GUANINA
9. MAIZE
10. MIRTO
11. MADRESELVA
12. MALAMBRE
13. PARA MI
14. PENDUEVA
15. UVANCILLO

ORUNLA'S SPIRITUAL POWER BATH

This bath is intended for Spiritualists and Santeros to bring them supernatural divination powers.

INGREDIENTS

1. MIRTO
2. AGUA DE COCO
3. FLORIDA WATER
4. RAIN WATER
5. ACHE DE SANTO
6. GREEN / YELLOW CANDLE

PREPARATION

1. Boil the Mirto and Ache de Santo in 1 gallon of water.
2. Allow the mixture to cool.
3. Strain the liquid from the mixture into a large bowl.
4. Add the Agua de Coco to the liquid mixture.
5. Add the Florida Water to the liquid mixture.
6. Light the candle in honor of Orunla.
7. Pour the liquid mixture into your bath water.

Remain in the bath water for 30 minutes. Some Santeros recommend adding water that has been charged with crystals to the bath water. Take this bath before seeing your clients.

OYA

The Orisha Oya is the Goddess of the Cemetery and the Winds. Baths using her sacred herbs are primarily for individuals who work as professional spiritualists

HERBS SACRED TO OYA

1. ALCANFOR
2. ARTESIMA
3. BARIA
4. BONITA
5. CIRUELA
6. CAMBIA VOZ
7. CABO DE HACHA

8. CAMITILLO
9. ESPANTA MUERTO
10. FLOR DE CEMENTERIO
11. FLAMBOYAN
12. GUARA
13. GERANIO
14. LLANTEN

15. MAZAORGUILLA
16. MARAVILLA
17. PALO CAJA
18. VARIA
19. VERGONZOSA
20. YUCA

OYA POWER BATH

This bath gives an individual great supernatural power and command to work with spirits.

INGREDIENTS

1. FLOR DE CEMENTERIO
2. ESPANTA MUERTO
3. RAIN WATER
4. VIOLET WATER
5. PURPLE CANDLE

PREPARATION

1. Boil the Flor de Cementerio and the Espanta Muerto in 1 gallon of water.
2. Allow the mixture to cool.
3. Strain the liquid from the mixture into a large bowl.
4. Add the Rain Water to the liquid mixture.
5. Add the Violet Water to the liquid mixture.
6. Light the candle in honor of Oya.
7. Pour the liquid mixture into your bath water.

Remain in the bath water for 30 minutes. This bath should be taken for 5 consecutive days for maximum power.

OYA PROTECTION BATH

This bath gives an individual the power to escape death.

INGREDIENTS

1. CIRUELA
2. PALO MUERTO
3. CASCARILLA
4. FLORIDA WATER
5. PURPLE CANDLE

PREPARATION

1. Boil the Ciruela and the Palo Muerto in one gallon of water.
2. Allow the mixture to cool.
3. Strain the liquid from the mixture into a large bowl.
4. Add the Cascarilla to the liquid mixture.
5. Add the Florida Water to the liquid mixture.
6. Light the candle in honor of Oya.
7. Pour the liquid mixture into your bath water.

Remain in the bath water for 30 minutes. This bath should be taken for five consecutive days. A very simple bath but extremely effective.

OCHOSI

In Santeria, the Orisha Ochosi is known as the "Great Hunter". Ochosi helps individuals fight legal matters and protects his followers from their enemies.

HERBS SACRED TO OCHOSI

1. ALBAHACA MORADA
2. ANAMU
3. ADORMIDERA
4. AMANSA GUAPO
5. CERCELERA
6. CANA SANTA
7. CHINCHA
8. ESPARTILLA
9. ESPINILBA
10. ESPANTA POLICIA
11. EBANA
12. HUESO DE GALLO
13. HIGUERTA
14. INCIENSO GUINEO
15. JIA BLANCA
16. PATA DE GALLINA
17. PARRAL
18. PALO MANAJU
19. PEGOJO
20. QUINTA MALDICION
21. ROMERO
22. SALVADER
23. SIEMPRE VIVA
24. TOBACCO
25. YERBA MORA
26. YERBA DE SANGRE

OCHOSI'S COURT BATH

This bath is used by an individual to win in court.

INGREDIENTS

1. ALBAHACA MORADA
2. ROMERO
3. ESPANTA POLICIA
4. SALVADERA
5. FLORIDA WATER
6. POLVO DE VENADO
7. PURPLE CANDLE

PREPARATION

1. Boil the Albahaca Morada, Romero, Salvadera and the Espanta Policia in one gallon of water.
2. Allow the mixture to cool.

3. Strain the liquid from the mixture into a large bowl.
4. Add the Florida Water to the liquid mixture.
5. Add the Cascarilla to the liquid mixture.
6. Add the Polvo de Venado to the liquid mixture.
7. Light the candle in honor of Ochosi.
8. Pour the liquid mixture into your bath water.

Remain in the bath water for 30 minutes. Take this bath for three consecutive days befor going to court.

OCHOSI'S JAIL BATH

This will help an individual avoid going to jail.

1. ROMERO
2. ALBAHACA MORADA
3. CASCARILLA
4. POLVO DE VENADO
5. QUINTA MALDICION
6. ANISETTE LIQUOR
7. WHITE CANDLE

PREPARATION

1. Boil the Romero, Albahaca Morada and the Quinta Maldicion in one gallon of water.
2. Allow the mixture to cool.
3. Strain the liquid from the mixture into a large bowl.
4. Add the Anisette Liquor to the liquid mixture.
5. Add half of the Polvo de Venado to the liquid mixture.
6. Light the candle in honor of Ochosi.
7. Pour the liquid mixture into your bath water.

Remain in the bath water for 30 minutes. This bath should be taken for seven consecutive days before going to court. On the day of court, take a small amount of Polvo de Venado and sprinkle it on the floor of the court room.

Ochosi's Escape The Law Bath

This bath is used by an individual to escape the law. Some Santeros say that this bath will virtually make an individual invisible so that they will to escape unnoticed by the naked eye.

INGREDIENTS

1. Yerba de Sangre
2. Pata de Gallina
3. Milk
4. Agua de Coco
5. Espanta Policia
6. Kolonia 1800
7. Cascarilla
8. Purple Candle

PREPARATION

1. Boil the Yerba de Sangre, Pata de Gallina and the Espanta Policia in one gallon of water.
2. Allow the mixture to cool.
3. Strain the liquid mixture into a large bowl.
4. Add the Agua de Coco to the liquid mixture.
5. Add the Milk to the liquid mixture.
6. Add the Kolonia 1800 to the liquid mixture.
7. Add the Cascarilla to the liquid mixture.
8. Light the candle in honor of Ochosi.
9. Pour the liquid mixture into your bath water.

Remain in your bath water for 30 minutes. Take this bath for three consecutive days. For extra protection it is recommended that you rub a cross on the bottom of both feet with the Cascarilla.

OGGUN

The Orisha Oggun protects individuals from dangerous accidents and tragedies. He is associated with policemen, soldiers, physicians and welders.

HERBS SACRED TO OGGUN

1. ANAMU
2. ADORMIDERA
3. ALMASIGO
4. BIBIJAGUA
5. CANA SANTA
6. CAMPANA MORADA
7. CALDO SANTO
8. ESCANDON
9. EBANO
10. AMANSA GUAPO
11. GUANBINA
12. GUAO
13. HIERBA HEDIONDA
14. HIGUERTA
15. HOJA DE ROBLE
16. HUESO DE GALLO
17. JIQUI
18. PIMIENTA ROJA
19. PIMIENTA NEGRA
20. PALO MANAJU
21. PALO BOMBA
22. PICHA DE GATO
23. PIGOJO
24. QUITA MALDICION
25. ROMERO
26. ROMPE ZARAGUEY
27. RABO DE PIEDRA
28. SIEMPRE VIVA
29. SALVADERA
30. UNA DE GATA
31. YERBA DE SANGRE
32. YERBA MORA
33. ZARZAPARILLA

OGGUN PROTECTION BATH #1

This bath protects an individual from danger and accidents while traveling.

INGREDIENTS

1. ROMERO
2. ZARZAPARILLA
3. SALVADERA
4. YERBA DE SANGRE
5. QUITA MALDICION
6. CASCARILLA
7. AGUA DE COCO
8. GREEN CANDLE

43

PREPARATION

1. Boil the Romero, Salvadera, Zarzaparilla, Yerba de Sangre and Quita Maldicion in one gallon of water.
2. Allow the mixture to cool.
3. Strain the liquid mixture into a large bowl.
4. Add the Agua de Coco to the liquid mixture.
5. Add the Cascarilla to the liquid mixture.
6. Light the candle in honor of Oggun.
7. Pour the liquid mixture into your bath water.

Remain in the bath water for 30 minutes. Take this bath before leaving on a trip.

OGGUN PROTECTION BATH #2

This bath is taken by an individual before a medical surgery to lessen the dangers.

INGREDIENTS

1. CAMPANA MORADA
2. AGUA DE COCO
3. CASCARILLA
4. KOLONIA 1800
5. SIEMPRE VIVA
6. PURPLE CANDLE

PREPARATION

1. Boil the Campana Morada and the Siempre Viva in one gallon of water.
2. Allow the mixture to cool.
3. Strain the liquid from the mixture into a large bowl.
4. Add the Agua de Coco to the liquid mixture.
5. Add the Cascarilla into the liquid mixture.
6. Add the Kolonia 1800 to the liquid mixture.
7. Light the candle in honor of Oggun.
8. Pour the liquid mixture into your bath water.

Remain in the bath water for 30 minutes. This bath should be taken for three consecutive days before a surgery.

OGGUN PROTECTION BATH #3

This bath should be used by an individual who feels that they are in danger of being the victim of violence or a crime.

INGREDIENTS

1. Yerba de Sangre
2. Caldo Santo
3. Adormidera
4. Cascarilla
5. Siete Machos Water
6. Green Candle

PREPARATION

1. Boil the Yerba de Sangre, Caldo Santo and the Adormidera in one gallon of water.
2. Allow the mixture to cool.
3. Strain the liquid from the mixture into a large bowl.
4. Add the Siete Machos Water to the liquid mixture.
5. Add the Cascarilla to the liquid mixture.
6. Light the candle in honor of Oggun.
7. Pour the liquid mixture into your bath.

Remain in the bath water for 30 minutes. Take bath as often as you feel the need.

OSAIN

The mighty and powerful Orisha Osain is the keeper of the sacred herbs. The Orisha Osain controls the forces of nature. Baths using the sacred herbs of Osain bring an individual supernatural power and stability.

HERBS SACRED TO OSAIN

1. ABRE CAMINO
2. ALCRANCILLO
3. ATEJE
4. ALMENDRA
5. ALAMO
6. ANIS
7. COLONIA
8. DIEZ DEL DIA
9. ESCOBA AMARGA
10. HIERBA NINA
11. FLOR DE CEMENTERIO
12. FLAMBOYAN
13. GALAN DE NOCHE
14. GUANINA
15. PARA MI
16. ROSA DE JERICO
17. SALVIA
18. TAPA CAMINO

OSAIN POWER BATH

This bath is used before performing a magic ritual or spell to bring the individual great supernatural powers.

INGREDIENTS

1. YERBA BUENA
2. FLOR DE CEMENTERIO
3. FLOR DE AGUA
4. FLOR DEL MAR
5. COLONIA
6. DIEZ DEL DIA
7. AGUA DE COCO
8. SIETE MACHOS WATER
9. SEVEN AFRICAN POWERS CANDLE

PREPARATION

1. Boil the Yerba Buena, Flor de Cementerio, Flor de Agua, Flor del Mar, Colonia and the Diez del Dia in one gallon of water.
2. Allow the mixture to cool.
3. Strain the liquid from the mixture into a large bowl.

4. Add the Agua de Coco to the liquid mixture.
5. Add the Siete Machos Water to the liquid mixture.
6. Light the candle in honor of Osain.
7. Allow the liquid mixture to stand for 24 hours.
8. After the 24 hours, pour the liquid mixture into your bath water.

Remain in the bath water for 30 minutes. Some Santeros recommend taking a small amount of the liquid mixture and sprinkling it in the four corners of the room where the ritual will take place.

SEVEN AFRICAN POWERS

Specifically the Seven African Powers are Obatala, Yemaya, Oshun, Chango, Orula, Ogun and Elegua. Each Orisha is identified with natural forces as well as with human interests or endeavors. These Orishas are mediators between humanity and the Supreme being.

SEVEN AFRICAN POWERS BATH #1

This bath is used for power and protection.

INGREDIENTS

1. SEVEN MULTI-COLORED ROSES
2. HOLY WATER
3. AGUA DE COCO
4. ACHE DE SANTO
5. RAIN WATER
6. AGUA DE NARANJA
7. SEVEN AFRICAN POWERS CANDLE

PREPARATION

1. Peel off the petals from the roses and cut them up into fine pieces.
2. Place the flower petals in a large bowl.
3. Add the Holy Water to the flower mixture.
4. Add the Agua de Coco to the flower mixture.
5. Boil the Ache de Santo in half a gallon of water.
6. Allow the mixture to cool.
7. Strain the Ache de Santo liquid into the large bowl with the other ingredients.
8. Light the candle in honor of the Seven African Powers.
9. Pour the liquid mixture into your bath water.

Remain in the bath water for 30 minutes.

SEVEN AFRICAN POWERS BATH #2

This bath is used for special requests and favors. This bath also protects and brings success to individuals.

INGREDIENTS

1. YERBA BUENA
2. ROSES
3. ROMERO
4. FLOR DE AGUA
5. SEA WATER
6. RIVER WATER
7. AGUA DE COCO
8. HOLY WATER
9. FLORIDA WATER
10. MANTECA DE COROJO
11. CASCARILLA
12. SEVEN AFRICAN POWERS CANDLE

PREPARATION

1. Boil the Romero, Yerba Buena and the Manteca de Corojo in one gallon of water.
2. Allow the mixture to cool.
3. Strain the liquid from the mixture into a large bowl.
4. Cut the Rose Petals and the Flor de Agua into small fine pieces.
5. Mix the flower pieces into the liquid mixture.
6. Add the Sea Water, River Water, Agua de Coco, Florida Water and the Holy Water to the liquid mixture.
7. Add the Cascarilla to the liquid mixture.
8. Light the candle in honor of the Seven African Powers.
9. Pour the liquid mixture into your bath water.

Remain in the bath water for 30 minutes. It is also recommended to anoint your body after your bath with Seven African Powers Spiritual Oil or the Ache de Santo Spiritual Oil.

CLEANSING BATHS

CLEANSING BATH #1

This bath is taken by an individual for clarity of mind.

INGREDIENTS

1. COCONUT
2. ACHE DE SANTO
3. HOLY WATER
4. CASCARILLA
5. AGUA DE FLORIDA

PREPARATION

1. Grate the meat of a coconut.
2. Place the grated coconut meat into a large bowl.
3. Mix the Holy Water, Agua de Florida and the Cascarilla into the bowl with the coconut.
4. Mix the Ache de Santo into the mixture.
5. Pour the mixture into the bath water.

Remain in the bath water for 30 minutes. This cleansing bath should be taken for three consecutive days.

CLEANSING BATH #2

This cleansing bath is used to purify the soul.

INGREDIENTS

1. WHITE CARNATIONS
2. CANELA
3. AGUA DE COCO
4. HOLY WATER
5. KOLONIA 1800
6. FLORIDA WATER

PREPARATION

1. Boil the Canela in one gallon of water.
2. Allow the liquid mixture to cool.

3. Strain the liquid mixture into a large bowl.
4. Peal the petals from the White Carnations.
5. Pour the Holy Water, Florida Water and the Agua de Coco into the liquid mixture.
6. Mix the White Carnation petals into the liquid mixture.
7. Pour the liquid mixture into your bath water.

Remain in the warm bath water for 30 minutes. This cleansing bath should be taken before going to bed. Many Santeros recommend adding Cascarilla to the liquid mixture.

RITUAL CLEANSING BATH

This bath is used to cleanse an individual after performing a ceremony or ritual.

INGREDIENTS

1. ACHE DE SANTO   4. HOLY WATER
2. GOAT'S MILK   5. PLUMA DE LORO
3. CASCARILLA

PREPARATION

1. Pour the Goat's Milk into a large bowl.
2. Mix the Holy Water with the Goat's Milk.
3. Mix the Ache de Santo and the Cascarilla to the Goat's Milk mixture.
4. Pour your bath water.
5. Carefully stand up in the bath tub and pour the mixture over your head.
6. Soak in the bath water for 30 minutes.
7. Rinse with water.
8. After drying off, rub your entire body with the Pluma de Loro.

SPIRITUAL POWER BATHS

Although the formulas are well guarded secrets of the Santero Priest, there exist powerful herbal baths that give a Spiritualist or Santero great supernatural powers. Included are a few of these secret bath formulas.

SANTERO POWER BATH

This bath can also be used by a male spiritualist or Santero.

INGREDIENTS

1. ABRE CAMINO
2. SALVADERA
3. SALVIA
4. PARAISO
5. MARAVILLA
6. AGUA DE COCO
7. SEA WATER
8. RAIN WATER
9. RIVER WATER
10. HOLY WATER
11. FLOR DE AGUA
12. CASCARILLA
13. KOLONIA
14. ACHE DE SANTO
15. 14 DAY SEVEN AFRICAN POWERS CANDLE

PREPARATION

1. Boil the Abre Camino, Salvadera, Paraiso, Salvia and Maravilla in one gallon of water.
2. Allow the mixture to cool.
3. Pour the Agua de Coco, Sea Water, River Water, Rain Water, Holy Water, Ache de Santo and the Kolonia 1800 to the liquid mixture.
4. Chop up the petals of the Flor de Agua.
5. Mix the prepared petals of the Flor de Agua
6. into the liquid mixture.
   Mix the Cascarilla to the liquid mixture.
7. Light the candle and place it next to the bowl.
8. Allow the mixture to remain in a cool place for 21 days, you may then add it to your bath.

Remain in the bath water for 30 minutes. Light a White Candle when you take your bath.

SANTERA POWER BATH

This bath is for women only.

INGREDIENTS

1. ABRE CAMINO
2. HOJA DE GUAYABA
3. ROMERO
4. RUDA
5. YERBA BUENA
6. WHITE ROSES
7. AGUA DE COCO
8. RIVER WATER
9. RAIN WATER
10. SEA WATER
11. AGUA DE ROSES
12. KOLONIA 1800
13. CASCARILLA
14. CANELA
15. 14 DAY WHITE CANDLE

PREPARATION

1. Boil the Abre Camino, Hoja de Guayaba, Romero, Ruda, Yerba Buena and the Canela in one gallon of water.
2. Allow the mixture to cool.
3. Strain the liquid fromthe mixture into a large bowl.
4. Pour the Agua de Coco, Agua de Rosa, Sea Water, Rain Water and the Kolonia 1800 into the liquid mixture.
5. Chop up the petals of the White Roses and add them to the liquid mixture.
6. Mix the Cascarilla into the liquid mixture.
7. Light the White Candle and place it next to the liquid mixture.
8. Place the liquid mixture in a cool place and allow to stand for 14 days, you may then pour the mixture into your bath water.

Remain in the bath water for 30 minutes.

SPIRITUALIST POWER BATH

This bath is used by spiritualists and Mediums of Santeria to enhance their communication with the spirit world.

INGREDIENTS

1. CARNATIONS
2. HONEY
3. MILK
4. HOLY WATER
5. FLORIDA WATER
6. POLVO HUESO DE MUERTO
7. PURPLE CANDLE

PREPARATION

1. Light the Purple Candle.
2. Mix the Milk, Honey and the Agua de Florida into a large bowl.
3. Pour the mixture into your bath water.
4. Chop the Carnation Petals into fine pieces.
5. Pour the Holy Water into the flower mixture.
6. Mix the Cascarilla with the flower mixture.
7. While taking your bath with the milk mixture, pour the mixture over your head.

Soak in the bath water for 30 minutes. Take this bath whenever there is a full moon. This bath gives incredible powers and discernment to a Spiritualist. The Polvo Hueso de Muerto should be applied to the palms of both hands and to the forehead in the form of a cross.

PALO MAYOMBE

Within the complex Orisha Religion, there exists a dark side of Santeria. The individuals are called Paleros. Paleros work with spiritually earthbound dark spirits. A Palero possesses a great amount of knowledge in the art of black magic. It can be used for both good and evil.

PALERO POWER BATH

INGREDIENTS

1. POLVO DE LOS MUERTOS
2. POLVO DE GANGA
3. FLOR DE CEMETERO
4. ABRE CAMINO
5. AGUARDIENTE
6. PALO RAMON
7. PALO GUAMA
8. KOLONIA 1800
9. RED CANDLE

PREPARATION

1. In one gallon of water, boil the Abre Camino, Flor de Cemeterio, Palo Ramon and the Palo Guama.
2. Allow the mixture to cool.
3. Strain the liquid from the mixture into a large bowl.
4. Mix the Polvo de los Muertos and the Polvo de Ganga into the liquid mixture.
5. Pour the Aguardiente and the Kolonia 1800 into the liquid mixture.
6. Light the Red Candle in honor of the Spirits of Palo Mayombe.
7. Pour your bath water.
8. While standing in the bath tub, carefully pour the mixture over your head.
9. Soak in the bath water for 30 minutes.

Most Paleros of the Montenegro Family recommend using a black candle instead of a red candle if you will be working with extremely powerful dark spirits. This bath gives incredible supernatural power and it should only be used by experienced Paleros or a High Priest of the Black Magic Arts.

WARNING: Do not take this bath before 6:00 P.M.

PALERO CLEANSING BATH

Immediately after performing a ritual or ceremony in Palo Mayombe, an individual must take a special cleansing bath to purify themselves from negative vibrations.

INGREDIENTS

1. GOAT'S MILK
2. LIME JUICE
3. SANTERIA KOSHER ROCK SALT

4. RUDA
5. HOLY WATER
6. POMEGRANATE JUICE

PREPARATION

1. Boil the Ruda in one gallon of water.
2. Allow the mixture to cool.
3. Strain the liquid from the mixture into a large bowl.
4. Pour the Holy Water, Pomegranate Juice and the Lime Juice into the liquid mixture.
5. Mix the Santeria Kosher Rock Salt into the liquid mixture.
6. Pour the Goat's Milk into the liquid mixture.
7. Pour the entire liquid mixture into your bath water.

Remain in the bath water for 30 minutes.

MEXICAN SPIRITUAL BATHS
THE ANCIENT ART OF MEXICAN WITCHCRAFT

SANTO NINO ATOCHA

This bath is used to open up the doors to opportunity and success. Santo Nino Atocha is associated in Santeria with Eleggua. Many individuals use the spiritual forces of Santo Nino Atocha when they are seeking employment. This Catholic Saint is one of the most powerful Mexican Witches.

INGREDIENTS

1. ABRE CAMINO
2. YERBA BUENA
3. NOPALES
4. AGUADE SIETE MACHOS
5. RED CANDLE

PREPARATION

1. In one gallon of water, boil the Abre Camino, the Nopales and the Yerba Buena.
2. Allow the mixture to cool.
   Strain the liquid from the mixture
3. into a large bowl.
   Pour the Agua de Siete Machos and the
4. Holy Water into the liquid mixture.
5. Light the Red Candle in honor of Santo Nino Atocha.
6. Pour the liquid mixture into your bath water.

Remain in the bath water for 30 minutes. For the best results, Mexican Witches recommend placing a small dish of candies and a picture of Santo Nino Atocha next to the candle. Santo Nino Atocha is said to be fond of candies and sweets.

JUSTO JUEZ COURT BATH

Justo Juez is known in Santeris as the Just Judge. Justo Juez protects individuals in court and from legal problems.

INGREDIENTS

1. MIRTO
2. AGUA DE SIETE MACHOS
3. ROMERO
4. AGUA DE NARANJA
5. HOLY WATER
6. WHITE CANDLE

PREPARATION

1. Boil the Mirto and the Ruda in one gallon of water.
2. Allow the mixture to cool.
3. Strain the liquid from the mixture into a large bowl.
4. Pour the Agua de Siete Machos, Agua de Naranja and the Holy Water into the liquid mixture.
5. Light the White Candle in Honor of Justo Juez.
6. Pour the liquid mixture into your bath water.

Remain in the bath water for 30 minutes. This bath should be taken seven consecutive days before going to court.

SANTO NINO FIDENCIO CONSTANTINO

Santo Nino Fidencio Constantino is a Folkloric Saint of Mexico's powerful Curanderos. He was a faith healer who lived among the people of Northern Mexico. During his short lifetime, Santo Nino Fidencio Constantino healed thousands of people from many terminal and incurable illnesses. These cases have been documented, but the Mexican government has tried to keep a tight seal on his life and miracles. Santo Nino Fidencio Constantino died in the 1960's. In Mexico, Spiritualists and Curanderos (Faith Healers) call upon the powers of his spirit to assist them in healing and helping people. Even to this very day, miracles are performed in Santo Nino Fidencio's name. Each year thousands of people make the long pilgramage to the town where he performed miracles in the name of God.

SANTO NINO FIDENCIO CONSTANTINO HEALING SPIRITUAL BATH

This is a popular version of the bath used by Mexican Curandero's carrying on the traditions of Santo Nino Fidencio Constantino to heal sickness and terminal illnesses.

INGREDIENTS

1. HOLY WATER
2. MIRTO
3. HOJA DE LIMON
4. 3 SMALL BRANCHES
   OF RUDA
5. SAGE
6. ROMERO
7. EUCALYPTUS OIL
8. AZTEC HERBAL
   HEALING OINTMENT

PREPARATION

1. Boil the Mirto, Sage, Hoja de Limon and the Romero in one gallon of water.
2. Allow the mixture to cool.
3. Strain the liquid from the mixture
4. into a large bowl.
   Pour the Holy Water into the liquid mixture.

59

5. Light the White Candle in honor of the
   Spirit of Santo Nino Fidencio Constantino.
6. Pour the liquid mixture into your bath water.
7. Remain in the bath water for 30 minutes.
8. After the bath, take the Ruda and brush and
   sweep your entire body with it from head to toe.
9. Take the Ruda and burn it in a fire.
10. Anoint your forehead with the
    Eucalyptus Oil in the form of a cross.
11. Before going to bed the same day, rub
    your body with the Aztec Healing Ointment.

*This bath should be taken for seven consecutive days. The Aztec Herbal
Healing Ointment is a very rare powerful ancient formula of magical
herbs used by Aztec Priests to heal.*

SANTO NINO FIDENCIO CONSTANTINO SPIRITUALIST BATH

This bath is used by Mexican Curanderos to receive
supernatural powers to heal people.

INGREDIENTS

1. SEMILLAS DE MAUSTAZO
2. AGUA DE ROSAS
3. HOLY WATER
4. 7 QUARTZ CRYSTALS
5. PURPLE OR GOLD CANDLE
6. KOSHER ROCK SALT

PREPARATION

1. In a large bucket, pour 5 gallons of Holy Water.
2. Add the Agua de Rosas to the Holy Water.
3. Place the 7 Quartz Crystals into the bucket.
4. Draw a circle around the outer edges of
   the bucket using the Kosher Rock Salt.
5. Light the candle and set next to the bucket.
6. Let the liquid mixture stand for 24 hours.

7. After the 24 hours, remove the crystals from the bucket.
8. Pour the liquid mixture into your bath water.

Remain in the bath water for 30 minutes. This bath should be taken by a healer before a ritual or ceremony.

SAN MARTIN CABALLERO

San Martin Caballero is known in Mexico as the "Champion of Business". Alters to San Martin Caballero can be found throughout Mexico in every home and business.

SAN MARTIN CABALLERO MONEY BATH

This bath is used by an individual who is involved in business. The bath's powers are said to shower an individual with money, wealth and success.

INGREDIENTS

1. PARAISO
2. PERJUL
3. HOLY WATER
4. AGUA DE FLORIDA
5. RED CANDLE

PREPARATION

1. In one gallon of water boil the Paraiso and the Perjil.
2. Allow the mixture to cool. Strain the liquid from the mixture into
3. a large bowl. Pour the Holy Water and the Agua
4. de Florida into the liquid mixture. Light the Red Candle in honor of
5. San Martin Caballero. Place the bowl containing the liquid mixture and the candle next to a picture or a statue
6. of St. Martin Caballero.
7. Allow the mixture to stand for 24 hours.
8. After the 24 hours, pour the liquid mixture into your bath water.

Remain in the bath water for 30 minutes. This bath should be taken for seven consecutive days. You will be amazed how fast the money starts rolling in.

SAN MARTIN DE PORRES

San Martin de Porres is a very popular and respected Catholic Saint in Mexico as well as in other Latin American countries. San Martinde Porres was born in Peru during the Spanish coloial occupation of Latin America. He was said to possess great supernatural powers such as telepathy, levitation and bilocation.

ST. MARTIN DE PORRES PSYCHIC BATH

Mexican witches use this bath in honor of San Martin de Porres to give them great supernatural powers and psychic abilities.

INGREDIENTS

1. WHITE ROSES   5. AGUA DE NARANJA
2. LILAC FLOWERS   6. HOLY WATER
3. AGUA DE LAVANDA   7. 7 DAY CANDLE
4. ABRE CAMINO

PREPARATION

1. Boil the Abre Camino, Lilac Flowers and petals from the White Roses in one gallon of water.
2. Allow the mixture to cool.
3. Pour the Agua de Lavanda, Agua de Naranja and the Holy Water into the liquid mixture.
4. Light the candle in honor of San Martin de Porres.
5. Place the bowl containing the liquid mixture and the candle next to a picture or a statue of San Martin de Porres.
6. Allow the mixture to stand for seven days or as long as the candle burns.
7. After the seven days, pour the liquid into your bath water.

Remain in the bath water for 30 minutes. Mexican Witches recommend taking this bath for nine consecutive nights. Nine gallons of this bath can be prepared at the same time and used over a nine day period.

SANTISIMA MUERTE

The Santisima Muerte is perhaps the most powerful and strongest Saint of the Mexican Witch. The Santisima Muerte is the guardian of death and the cemetery. The secrets and the mysteries of the Santisima Muerte are received in an initiation ceremony that takes place at night in a cemetery. The powers of the Santisima Muerte are used in such spells as love, business and, of course, black magic. When an individual has been initiated into the mysteries of the Santisima Muerte, they are empowered with great spiritual command and supernatural powers.

SANTISIMA MUERTE SUPERNATURAL POWER BATH

This bath is used by individuals working with the forces of darkness. This bath will give you the extra spiritual energy needed in accomplishing your magic spells.

INGREDIENTS

1. FLOR DE CEMETERIO
2. POLVO DE LOS MUERTOS
3. ABRE CAMINO
4. PALO SUERTE
5. AGUA DE SIETE MACHOS
6. BLACK CANDLE

PREPARATION

1. Light the Black Candle in honor of the Santisima Muerte.
2. Boil the Flor de Cemeterio, Abre Camino and the Palo Muerto in one gallon of water.
3. Allow the mixture to stand for 24 hours.
4. After the 24 hours, strain the liquid from the mixture into a large bowl.
5. Pour the Agua de Siete Machos into the liquid mixture.
6. Pour the liquid mixture into your bath water.

Remain in the bath for 30 minutes. When you have finished your bath and have completely dried off, rub the Polvo de los Muertos in the form of a cross on the palms of both hands. The Polvo de los Muertos is used in order to have command over the dark spirits.

SANTISIMA MUERTE LOVE BATH

This bath uses the powers of the Santisima Muerte to attract a lover. Be careful, this one is strong.

INGREDIENTS

1. FLOR DE CEMETERIO
2. CANELA
3. PALO DE AMANSA GUAPO
4. PALO DE BRAZIL
5. VIOLET WATER
6. RED CANDLE

PREPARATION

1. Boil the Palo de Amnsa Guapo, Palo de Brazil, Flor de Cemeterio, Canela and the Abre Camino in one gallon of water.
2. Allow the mixture to cool.
3. Strain the liquid from the mixture into a large bowl.
4. Pour the Violet Water into the liquid mixture.
5. Light the Red Candle in honor of the Santisima Muerte.
6. Allow the liquid mixture to remain for 7 days.
7. After the 7 days, pour the liquid mixture into your bath water.

Remain in the bath water for 30 minutes. The bath should be taken for seven consecutive nights.

SAN SIMON

The powers of the most Honorable San Simon are widely known throughout Central and South America. San Simonis a Folkloric Saint from Guatemala. He has been given the name "Protector of the Hopeless". He has been associated with the protection of the extreme poor and impoverished individuals, prostitutes, homosexuals and criminals. The following baths to San Simon are versions used by Central American Witches, particularly in Nicaragua where the world's strongest and most powerful black magic is practiced. Many Paleros would not be able to compete with this powerful jungle magic.

SAN SIMON PROTECTION BATH

This bath is used by individuals for protection and power over their enemies.

INGREDIENTS

1. RUDA
2. SUGAR CANE
3. MILK
4. POLVO DE LAS TORTUGAS
5. POLVO DE LOS INDIOS
6. HOLY WATER
7. SEVEN AFRICAN POWERS CANDLE
8. BLACK ROOSTER

PREPARATION

1. Cut a 12 inch piece of Sugar Cane into small pieces.
2. Boil the Sugar Cane pieces and the Ruda in one gallon of water.
3. Allow the mixture to cool.
4. Strain the liquid from the mixture into a large bowl.
5. Pour the Milk, Holy Water and the Aguardiente into the liquid mixture.
6. Light the 7 African Powers Candle in honor of San Simon.

7. Add the Polvo de los Indios and the Polvos de las Tortugas to the liquid mixture.
8. Place the bowl with the liquid mixture and the candle next to a statue or a picture of San Simon. Offer the Black Rooster to San Simon and
9. ask for his assistance. Cut the head off the rooster and let the blood drip onto the statue of San Simon and also into the liquid mixture.
10. Pour the liquid mixture into your bath water.

Remain in the bath water for 30 minutes. This bath should be taken at night before going to bed.

SAN SIMON'S COURT BATH

This bath is used by an individual to win in court. This bath is very strong and should be taken at night before going to bed.

INGREDIENTS

1. ROMERO	5. HOJAS DE PLANTANO
2. HOLY WATER	6. RED CANDLE
3. 7 GREEN LIMES	7. POLVO DE LEON
4. AGUA DE COCO	

PREPARATION

1. Light the red candle in honor of San Simon.
2. Slice up the limes and the Hoja de Plantano into fine pieces.
3. Boil the Romero and the Limes in one gallon of water.
4. Allow the mixture to cool.
5. Pour the Holy Water and the Agua de Coco into the liquid mixture.
6. Invoke the name of San Simon to assist you in court.
7. Pour the liquid into your bath water.

(continued)

Remain in the bath water for 30 minutes. Take this bath before going to bed. On the day of court, drop the Polvo de Leon in front of the court house where your trial will be held.

SAN SIMON'S LOVE BATH

This bath is used to attract love or marriage. Central American Witches claim that although this bath is very simple, it is effective and very powerful.

INGREDIENTS

1. Palo de Amansa Guapo
2. Abre Camino
3. Canela
4. Agua de Coco
5. Aguardiente
6. Female Image Candle (Red)
7. Male Image Candle (Red)
8. Holy Water
9. Honey

PREPARATION

1. Boil the Palo de Amansa Guapo, Canela and the Abre Camino in one gallon of water.
2. Allow the mixture to cool.
3. Mix the Agua de Coco and the Holy Water with the liquid mixture.
4. Carve your name on the candle that represents you three times.
5. Place the two candles facing each other and tie them together with red thread.
6. Light the two candles and invoke the name of San Simon asking him to send you a lover.
7. Pour the liquid mixture into your bath water.
8. Wash yourself with the Honey.

Remain in the bath water for 30 minutes. Allow the candles to completely burn out. This bath should be taken for five consecutive days before leaving the house daily. Be careful what you ask for because you will get it.

Item #039
$16.95

SANTERIA
FORMULARY & SPELLBOOK
CANDLES • HERBS• INCENSE • OILS
A GUIDE TO NATURE'S MAGIC

CARLOS MONTENEGRO

The belief in natural magic is shared by millions who are participants of the Afro Caribbean religion known as Santeria. This book was written as a *"How to"* guide for individuals who are active participants in the Santeria Religion. It's purpose is to introduce and encourage individuals of Santeria to familiarize themselves with an inexpensive way of preparing basic ingredients to produce "natural magic". Rarely is careful attention paid to the preparation of homemade magic products in these modern times. Rarer still, is finding an individual who is dedicated and competent in this aspect of spellcrafting. It is a magical institution that is dying and must not be overlooked or forgotten. Making homemade products is a lengthy process, but the success of a magical spell or ritual demands patience and faith. This book is an important resource guide to the magic found within nature. If properly utilized with respect and reverence, the Santeria practitioner will live harmoniously in nature with the Orishas.

ISBN 0-942272-52-8   5½"x 8½"

Toll Free: 1 (888) OCCULT - 1

ITEM #001
$12.95

SANTERIA
AFRICAN MAGIC
IN LATIN AMERICA

By Migene Gonzalez Wippler

In 1973, the first hardcover edition of *Santeria: African Magic in Latin America* by cultural anthropologist Migene Gonzalez-Wippler was first published by Julian Press. It became an immediate best-seller and is still considered by many experts one of the most popular books on Santeria, having gone through 4 editions and several translations. Now this beloved classic, written by one the foremost scholars on the Afro-Cuban religion, has returned in a 5th edition. This time the text has been carefully edited and corrected to incorporate vital new material. The beliefs, practices, legends of Santeria are brilliantly brought to life in this exciting and critically acclaimed best-seller. If you ever wondered what Santeria is, if you are curious about the rituals and practices of this mysterious religion, and want to delve in its deepest secrets, this book will answer all your questions and much more.

ISBN 0-942272-04-8 5½"x 8½" $12.95

Toll Free: 1 (888) OCCULT - 1

Item #005
$9.95

POWERS OF THE ORISHAS
Santeria and the Worship of Saints
Migene Gonzalez Wippler

Santeria is the Afro-Cuban religion based on an amalgamation between some of the magio-religious beliefs and practices of the Yoruba people and those of the Catholic church. In Cuba where the Yoruba proliferated extensively, they became known as *Lucumi,* a word that means "friendship".

Santeria is known in Cuba as Lucumi Religion. The original Yoruba language, interspersed with Spanish terms and corrupted through the centuries of misuse and mispronunciation, also became known as Lucumi. Today some of the terms used in Santeria would not be recognized as Yoruba in Southwestern Nigeria, the country of origin of the Yoruba people.

Santeria is a Spanish term that means a confluence of saints and their worship. These saints are in reality clever disguises for some of the Yoruba deities, known as Orishas. During the slave trade, the Yoruba who were brought to Cuba were forbidden the practice of their religion by their Spanish masters. In order to continue their magical and religious observances safely the slaves opted for the identification and disguise of the Orishas with some of the Catholic saints worshipped by the Spaniards. In this manner they were able to worship their deities under the very noses of the Spaniards without danger of punishment.

Throughout the centuries the practices of the Yoruba became very popular and soon many other people of the Americas began to practice the new religion.

ISBN 0-942272-25-0   5½"x 8½"   144 pages $9.95
Toll Free: 1 (888) OCCULT - 1

ORIGINAL PUBLICATIONS

- [ ] **HELPING YOURSELF WITH SELECTED PRAYERS**; *Volume 1*; $7.95
- [ ] **HELPING YOURSELF WITH SELECTED PRAYERS**: *Volume 2*; $9.95
- [ ] **ORIGINAL PUBLICATIONS COMPLETE BATH BOOK** - Canizares - $8.95
- [ ] **UNHEXING AND JINX REMOVING**; by Donna Rose - $5.95
- [ ] **SUCCESS AND POWER THROUGH PSALMS**; by Donna Rose - $5.95
- [ ] **DREAM YOUR LUCKY LOTTERY NUMBERS**; Canizares $5.95
- [ ] **PSALM WORKBOOK**: Robert Laremy - $7.95
- [ ] **SPIRITUAL CLEANSINGS & PSYCHIC PROTECTION**; Robert Laremy $8.95
- [ ] **READING YOUR FUTURE IN THE CARDS**; Eden - $6.95
- [ ] **NEW REVISED MASTER BOOK OF CANDLEBURNING**; Gamache - $7.95
- [ ] **THE MAGIC CANDLE**; Charmaine Dey $6.95
- [ ] **NEW REV. 6&7 BKS. OF MOSES**; Wippler $9.95
- [ ] **MYSTERY OF THE LONG LOST 8,9,10TH BOOKS OF MOSES**; Gamache - $7.95
- [ ] **VOODOO & HOODOO**; by Jim Haskins - $16.95
- [ ] **COMPLETE BOOK OF VOODOO**: Robert Pelton $16.95
- [ ] **PAPA JIM'S HERBAL MAGIC WORKBOOK**; Papa Jim - $7.95
- [ ] **HELPING YOURSELF WITH MAGICAL OILS A-Z**; Maria Solomon - $8.95
- [ ] **LOVE CHARMS & SPELLS**; Jade $6.95
- [ ] **MONEY MAGIC**; by Jade - $6.95
- [ ] **PROTECTION CHARMS & SPELLS**; Jade - $5.95
- [ ] **SANTERIA; AFRICAN MAGIC IN LATIN AMERICA**; Wippler $12.95
- [ ] **SANTERIA EXERIENCE**; Wippler $12.95
- [ ] **RITUALS AND SPELLS OF SANTERIA**; Wippler $9.95
- [ ] **MAGICAL HERBAL BATHS OF SANTERIA**; Carlos Montenegro $7.95
- [ ] **POWERS OF THE ORISHAS**; Wippler $9.95
- [ ] **THE BOOK ON PALO**; Raul Canizares $21.95
- [ ] **BRAZILIAN PALO PRIMER**: Robert Laremy $6.95
- [ ] **AGANJU; The Orisha of Volcanoes & Wilderness**; Canizares $5.95
- [ ] **ESHU ELLEGGUA; Santeria and the Orisha of the Crossroad**; Canizares $5.95
- [ ] **SHANGO; Santeria and the Orisha of Thunder**; Canizares $5.95
- [ ] **BABALU AYE; Santeria and the Lord of Pestilence**; Canizares $5.95
- [ ] **OSHUN: Santeria and the Orisha of Love**; Canizares $5.95
- [ ] **OGUN: Santeria and the Warrior Orisha of Iron**; Canizares $5.95
- [ ] **OYA: Santeria and the Orisha of Storms**; Canizares $5.95
- [ ] **YEMAYA: Santeria and the Orisha of the Seven Seas**; Canizares $5.95
- [ ] **ORUNLA: Santeria and the Orisha of Divination**; Canizares $5.95
- [ ] **OSANYIN: Santeria and the Orisha of Lord of Plants**; Canizares $5.95
- [ ] **OBATALA: Santeria and the White Robed King of the Orisha**; Canizares $5.95
- [ ] **AWO: IFA & THE THEOLOGY OF ORISHA DIVINATION**; Fatunmbi $19.95

NAME _____   TELEPHONE _____

ADDRESS _____

CITY _____   STATE _____   ZIP _____

 **TOLL FREE (888) 622-8581 -OR- (631) 420-4053**

TO ORDER BY MAIL: *CHECK THE BOXES NEXT TO YOUR SELECTIONS. ADD THE TOTAL. SHIPPING COSTS ARE $3.50 FOR THE FIRST BOOK PLUS 75 CENTS FOR EACH ADDITIONAL BOOK. NEW YORK STATE RESIDENTS PLEASE ADD 8.25% SALES TAX. ALL ORDERS SHIP IN 14 DAYS. SORRY, NO C.O.D.'S. SEND ORDERS TO THE ADDRESS BELOW.*

ORIGINAL PUBLICATIONS • P.O. BOX 236, OLD BETHPAGE, NY 11804-0236